SLIP 1, KNIT 1, PASS SLIPPED STITCH OVER

(abbreviated slip 1, K1, PSSO)
Slip one stitch as if to **knit**. Knit the next stitch. With the left needle, bring the slipped stitch over the knit stitch *(Fig. 4)* and off the needle.

Fig. 4

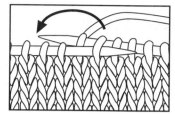

SLIP, SLIP, PURL *(abbreviated SSP)*

With yarn held in front of work, separately slip two stitches as if to **knit**. Place these two stitches back onto the left needle. Insert the **right** needle into the **back** of both stitches from **back** to **front** *(Fig. 5)*, then purl them together.

Fig. 5

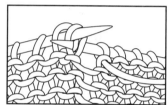

SLIP 1, KNIT 2 TOGETHER, PASS SLIPPED STITCH OVER

(abbreviated slip 1, K2 tog, PSSO)
Slip one stitch as if to **knit** *(Fig. 6a)*, then knit the next two stitches together. With the left needle, bring the slipped stitch over the stitch just made *(Fig. 6b)* and off the needle.

Fig. 6a

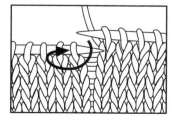

Fig. 6b

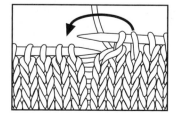

YARN C

After a knit

Bring the yarn
back **over** the
it is now in po

Fig. 7a

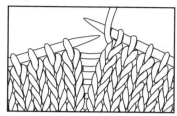

After a purl stitch, before a purl stitch

Take yarn **over** the right hand needle to the back, then forward **under** it, so that it is now in position to purl the next stitch *(Fig. 7b)*.

Fig. 7b

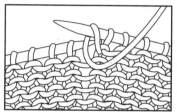

After a knit stitch, before a purl stitch

Bring yarn forward **between** the needles, then back **over** the top of the right hand needle and forward **between** the needles again, so that it is now in position to purl the next stitch *(Fig. 7c)*.

Fig. 7c

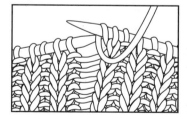

After a purl stitch, before a knit stitch

Take yarn **over** right hand needle to the back, so that it is now in position to knit the next stitch *(Fig. 7d)*.

Fig. 7d

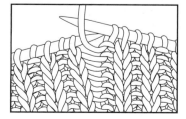

PICKING UP STITCHES

When instructed to pick up stitches, insert the needle from the **front** to the **back** under two strands at the edge of the worked piece *(Figs. 8a & b)*. Put the yarn around the needle as if to **knit**, then bring the needle with the yarn back through the stitch to the right side, resulting in a stitch on the needle.

Repeat this along the edge, picking up the required number of stitches.

A crochet hook may be helpful to pull yarn through.

Fig. 8a

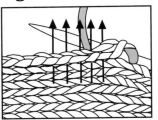

Fig. 8b

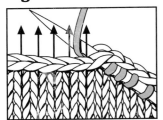

WEAVING SEAMS

With the **right** side of both pieces facing you and edges even, sew through both sides once to secure the seam. Insert the needle under the bar **between** the first and second stitches on the row and pull the yarn through *(Fig. 9)*. Insert the needle under the next bar on the second side. Repeat from side to side, being careful to match rows. If the edges are different lengths, it may be necessary to insert the needle under two bars at one edge.

Fig. 9

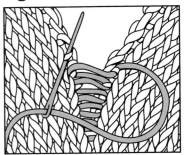

Production Team: Writer - Sarah J. Green; Technical Editor - Linda Luder; Artist - Chris Meux; and Photo Stylist - Sondra Daniel.

Layettes made and instructions tested by Anitta Armstrong, June Clevenger, Raymelle Greening, Vicki Kellogg, Kay Meadors, Dale Potter, Donna Soellner, and Margaret Taverner.

1. PERFECTLY PINK

Finished Size: 6 months

MATERIALS
Sacque, Bonnet, and Booties
Sport Weight Yarn:
  Sacque - 3½ ounces,
    (100 grams, 355 yards)
  Bonnet - ¾ ounce, (20 grams, 75 yards)
  Booties - ¾ ounce, (20 grams, 75 yards)
Straight knitting needles, sizes 4 (3.50 mm),
  5 (3.75 mm), **and** 6 (4.00 mm) **or** sizes
  needed for gauge ~~Use 3, 4 & 5~~
Stitch holders - 3
Tapestry needle
Sewing needle and thread
⅝" Buttons - 3
⅜"w Ribbon - 1 yard for Bonnet
Blanket
Worsted Weight Yarn:
  33 ounces, (940 grams, 1,925 yards)
  29" Circular knitting needles, sizes
    10½ (6.50 mm) **and** 11 (8.00 mm) **or**
    sizes needed for gauge

GAUGE: In pattern, with Sport Weight Yarn and
  larger size needles, 22 sts and 30 rows = 4"
  In pattern, with two strands of Worsted
  Weight Yarn and larger size circular
  needles, 13 sts and 19 rows = 4"

When instructed to slip a stitch, always slip as if to
knit.

SACQUE

Sacque is worked in one piece to underarm.

BODY
With medium size needles, cast on 120 sts.

Rows 1-5: Knit across.

Change to larger size needles.

Row 6 (Right side)**:** K8, YO *(Fig. 7a, page 2)*,
slip 1, K1, PSSO *(Fig. 4, page 2)*, (K4, YO, slip 1,
K1, PSSO) across to last 8 sts, K8.

Row 7: K4, purl across to last 4 sts, K4.

Row 8: K8, K2 tog *(Fig. 1, page 1)*, (YO, K4,
K2 tog) across to last 8 sts, YO, K8.

Row 9: K4, purl across to last 4 sts, K4.

Repeat Rows 6-9 for pattern until Sacque measures
approximately 7" from cast on edge, ending by
working Row 9.

RIGHT FRONT
Row 1 (Buttonhole row)**:** K2, **[YO, K2 tog
(buttonhole made)]**, (K4, YO, slip 1, K1, PSSO) 4
times, slip next 58 sts onto st holder (Back), slip
remaining 34 sts onto second st holder (Left Front):
28 sts.

Row 2: Purl across to last 4 sts, K4.

Row 3: K8, K2 tog, (YO, K4, K2 tog) twice, YO,
K3, K2 tog, K1: 27 sts.

Row 4: Purl across to last 4 sts, K4.

Row 5: K8, YO, slip 1, K1, PSSO, (K4, YO,
slip 1, K1, PSSO) twice, K2, K2 tog, K1: 26 sts.

Row 6: Purl across to last 4 sts, K4.

Row 7: K8, K2 tog, (YO, K4, K2 tog) twice, YO,
K1, K2 tog, K1: 25 sts.

Row 8: Purl across to last 4 sts, K4.

Row 9: K8, YO, slip 1, K1, PSSO, (K4, YO,
slip 1, K1, PSSO) twice, K3.

Row 10: Purl across to last 4 sts, K4.

Row 11: K8, K2 tog, (YO, K4, K2 tog) twice, YO,
K3.

Row 12: Purl across to last 4 sts, K4.

Row 13 (Buttonhole row)**:** K2, **[YO, K2 tog
(buttonhole made)]**, (K4, YO, slip 1, K1, PSSO) 3
times, K3.

Rows 14-16: Repeat Rows 10-12.

Rows 17-20: Repeat Rows 9-12.

Cut yarn.

NECK SHAPING
Row 1: Slip first 9 sts onto st holder, K5, YO,
slip 1, K1, PSSO, K4, YO, slip 1, K1, PSSO, K3:
16 sts.

Row 2: Purl across.

Row 3: K1, slip 1, K1, PSSO, K2, K2 tog, YO,
K4, K2 tog, YO, K3: 15 sts.

Row 4: Purl across.

Row 5: K1, slip 1, K1, PSSO, K1, YO, slip 1, K1,
PSSO, K4, YO, slip 1, K1, PSSO, K3: 14 sts.

Row 6: Purl across.

Row 7: K1, slip 1, K1, PSSO, K2 tog, YO, K4,
K2 tog, YO, K3: 13 sts.

Row 8: Purl across.

Row 9: K1, slip 1, K1, PSSO, K5, YO, slip 1, K1,
PSSO, K3: 12 sts.

Row 10: P9, SSP *(Fig. 5, page 2)*, P1: 11 sts.

Bind off remaining sts.

Continued on page 5.

BACK

With **right** side facing, slip 58 sts from Back st holder onto larger size needle.

Row 1: Bind off 6 sts (armhole), K3, (YO, slip 1, K1, PSSO, K4) across: 52 sts.

Row 2: Purl across.

Row 3: K1, slip 1, K1, PSSO, K1, K2 tog, (YO, K4, K2 tog) across to last 4 sts, YO, K1, K2 tog, K1: 50 sts.

Row 4: Purl across.

Row 5: K1, slip 1, K1, PSSO, YO, slip 1, K1, PSSO, (K4, YO, slip 1, K1, PSSO) across to last 3 sts, K2 tog, K1: 48 sts.

Row 6: Purl across.

Row 7: Slip 1, K1, PSSO, K2 tog, (YO, K4, K2 tog) across to last 2 sts, YO, K2 tog: 46 sts.

Row 8: Purl across.

Row 9: K1, YO, slip 1, K1, PSSO, (K4, YO, slip 1, K1, PSSO) across to last st, K1.

Row 10: Purl across.

Row 11: K1, K2 tog, (YO, K4, K2 tog) across to last st, YO, K1.

Rows 12-29: Repeat Rows 8-11, 4 times; then repeat Rows 8 and 9 once **more**.

Row 30: Bind off 11 sts, purl across.

Row 31: Bind off 11 sts, slip remaining 24 sts onto st holder.

LEFT FRONT

With **right** side facing, slip remaining 34 sts onto larger size needle.

Row 1: Bind off 6 sts (armhole), K5, YO, slip 1, K1, PSSO, (K4, YO, slip 1, K1, PSSO) twice, K8: 28 sts.

Row 2: K4, purl across.

Row 3: K1, slip 1, K1, PSSO, K3, K2 tog, (YO, K4, K2 tog) twice, YO, K8: 27 sts.

Row 4: K4, purl across.

Row 5: K1, slip 1, K1, PSSO, K2, YO, slip 1, K1, PSSO, (K4, YO, slip 1, K1, PSSO) twice, K8: 26 sts.

Row 6: K4, purl across.

Row 7: K1, slip 1, K1, PSSO, K1, K2 tog, (YO, K4, K2 tog) twice, YO, K8: 25 sts.

Row 8: K4, purl across.

Row 9: K3, YO, slip 1, K1, PSSO, (K4, YO, slip 1, K1, PSSO) twice, K8.

Row 10: K4, purl across.

Row 11: K3, K2 tog, (YO, K4, K2 tog) twice, YO, K8.

Rows 12-19: Repeat Rows 8-11 twice.

NECK SHAPING

Row 1: K4, P5, slip 9 sts just worked onto st holder, purl across: 16 sts.

Row 2: K3, YO, slip 1, K1, PSSO, K4, YO, slip 1, K1, PSSO, K5.

Row 3: Purl across.

Row 4: K3, K2 tog, YO, K4, K2 tog, YO, K2, K2 tog, K1: 15 sts.

Row 5: Purl across.

Row 6: K3, YO, slip 1, K1, PSSO, K4, YO, slip 1, K1, PSSO, K1, K2 tog, K1: 14 sts.

Row 7: Purl across.

Row 8: K3, K2 tog, YO, K4, K2 tog, YO, K2 tog, K1: 13 sts.

Row 9: Purl across.

Row 10: K3, YO, slip 1, K1, PSSO, K5, K2 tog, K1: 12 sts.

Row 11: P1, P2 tog **(Fig. 2, page 1)**, P9: 11 sts.

Bind off remaining sts.

SLEEVE (Make 2)
CUFF
With smaller size needles, cast on 32 sts **loosely**.

Rows 1-4: Knit across.

Row 5 (Increase row): Increase **(see Increases, page 1)**, knit across to last 2 sts, increase, K1: 34 sts.

BODY
Change to larger size needles.

Row 1 (Right side): K4, (YO, slip 1, K1, PSSO, K4) across.

Row 2: Purl across.

Row 3: K4, (K2 tog, YO, K4) across.

Row 4: Purl across.

Rows 5-10: Repeat Rows 1-4 once, then repeat Rows 1 and 2 once **more**.

Row 11 (Increase row): Increase, K3, K2 tog, (YO, K4, K2 tog) across to last 4 sts, YO, K2, increase, K1: 36 sts.

Maintaining established pattern, continue to increase one stitch at **each** edge, every tenth row, 2 times **more**: 40 sts.

Work even until Sleeve measures approximately 6" from cast on edge, ending by working a **purl** row.

5

SLEEVE CAP

Maintain established pattern throughout.

Rows 1 and 2: Bind off 3 sts, work across: 34 sts.

Row 3 (Decrease row)**:** K1, slip 1, K1, PSSO, work across to last 3 sts, K2 tog, K1: 32 sts.

Row 4: Purl across.

Rows 5-9: Repeat Rows 3 and 4 twice, then repeat Row 3 once **more**: 26 sts.

Rows 10-12: Work across.

Row 13 (Decrease row)**:** K1, slip 1, K1, PSSO, work across to last 3 sts, K2 tog, K1: 24 sts.

Rows 14-25: Repeat Rows 10-13, 3 times: 18 sts.

Rows 26 and 27: Bind off 4 sts, work across: 10 sts.

Bind off remaining sts.

FINISHING

Sew shoulder seams.

Weave underarm seam on each Sleeve *(Fig. 9, page 3)*.

Set in Sleeves, matching center of Row 27 on Sleeve to shoulder seam and easing to fit opening.

NECK BAND

Row 1: With **right** side facing, slip 9 sts from Right Front st holder onto smaller size needle and knit across, pick up 10 sts along Right Front neck edge *(Figs. 8a & b, page 3)*, slip 24 sts from Back st holder onto empty needle and knit across, pick up 10 sts along Left Front neck edge, slip 9 sts from Left Front st holder onto empty needle and knit across: 62 sts.

Rows 2-4: Knit across.

Row 5 (Buttonhole row)**:** K2, YO, K2 tog, knit across.

Rows 6-8: Knit across.

Bind off all sts **loosely** in **knit**.

Sew buttons to Left Front.

BONNET
CROWN

With medium size needles, cast on 62 sts.

Rows 1-7: Knit across.

Change to larger size needles.

Row 8 (Right side)**:** K3, YO *(Fig. 7a, page 2)*, slip 1, K1, PSSO *(Fig. 4, page 2)*, (K4, YO, slip 1, K1, PSSO) across to last 3 sts, K3.

Row 9: Purl across.

Row 10: K3, K2 tog *(Fig. 1, page 1)*, (YO, K4, K2 tog) across to last 3 sts, YO, K3.

Row 11: Purl across.

Rows 12-35: Repeat Rows 8-11, 6 times.

BACK

Row 1: Bind off 20 sts, YO, slip 1, K1, PSSO, (K4, YO, slip 1, K1, PSSO) across to last 3 sts, K3: 42 sts.

Row 2: Bind off 20 sts, purl across: 22 sts.

Row 3: K1, K2 tog, (YO, K4, K2 tog) 3 times, YO, K1.

Row 4: Purl across.

Row 5: K1, YO, slip 1, K1, PSSO, (K4, YO, slip 1, K1, PSSO) 3 times, K1.

Row 6: Purl across.

Rows 7-30: Repeat Rows 3-6, 6 times.

Slip sts onto st holder; cut yarn.

Sew sides of Back to bound off edges of Crown.

NECK BAND

Row 1: With **right** side facing and using smaller size needles, pick up 20 sts along first side of Crown *(Figs. 8a & b, page 3)*, slip 22 sts from Back st holder onto empty needle and knit across, pick up 20 sts along second side of Crown: 62 sts.

Row 2: Knit across.

Row 3: K 20, K2 tog 11 times, K 20: 51 sts.

Rows 4-8: Knit across.

Bind off all sts in **knit**.

Sew an 18" length of ribbon to each corner of Bonnet for tie. Trim as desired.

Continued on page 7.

BOOTIES

CUFF

With medium size needles, cast on 36 sts.

Rows 1-5: Knit across.

Change to larger size needles.

Row 6 (Right side)**:** K2, YO *(Fig. 7a, page 2)*, slip 1, K1, PSSO *(Fig. 4, page 2)*, (K4, YO, slip 1, K1, PSSO) 5 times, K2.

Row 7: Purl across.

Row 8: K2, K2 tog *(Fig. 1, page 1)*, (YO, K4, K2 tog) 5 times, YO, K2.

Row 9: Purl across.

Rows 10-17: Repeat Rows 6-9 twice.

Change to smaller size needles.

Rows 18-25: (K1, P1) across.

INSTEP

Change to larger size needles.

Row 1: K 13, slip sts just worked onto st holder, K 10, slip remaining 13 sts onto second st holder: 10 sts.

Beginning with a **purl** row, work 13 rows in Stockinette Stitch.

Slip sts onto st holder; cut yarn.

SIDES

With **right** side facing, slip 13 sts from first st holder onto larger size needle, pick up 7 sts along first side of Instep *(Figs. 8a & b, page 3)*, slip 10 sts from Instep st holder onto empty needle and knit across, pick up 7 sts along second side of Instep, slip 13 sts from last st holder onto empty needle and knit across: 50 sts.

Beginning with a **purl** row, work in Stockinette Stitch for 6 rows.

Decrease Row: P 20, P2 tog *(Fig. 2, page 1)*, P6, P2 tog, P 20: 48 sts.

SOLE

Row 1: K 27, K2 tog, leave remaining 19 sts unworked, **turn**.

Rows 2-31: K7, K2 tog, leave remaining sts unworked, **turn**.

Row 32: K7, K2 tog, knit remaining 4 sts: 16 sts.

Bind off all sts in **knit**.

Weave back seam *(Fig. 9, page 3)*.

Sew back of Sole to Sides.

BLANKET

Finished Size: 36" x 45"

Blanket is worked holding two strands of yarn together.

With smaller size circular needles, cast on 118 sts.

Rows 1-5: Knit across.

Change to larger size circular needles.

Row 6 (Right side)**:** K4, ★ YO *(Fig. 7a, page 2)*, slip 1, K1, PSSO *(Fig. 4, page 2)*, K4; repeat from ★ across.

Row 7: K4, purl across to last 4 sts, K4.

Row 8: K4, ★ K2 tog *(Fig. 1, page 1)*, YO, K4; repeat from ★ across.

Row 9: K4, purl across to last 4 sts, K4.

Repeat Rows 6-9 for pattern until Blanket measures approximately 44" from cast on edge, ending by working a **right** side row.

Change to smaller size circular needles.

Last 5 Rows: Knit across.

Bind off all sts.

2. BELOVED BLUE

Finished Size: 6 months

MATERIALS
Sacque, Bonnet, and Booties
Sport Weight Yarn:
  Sacque - 3¾ ounces,
    (110 grams, 380 yards)
  Bonnet - ¾ ounce, (20 grams, 75 yards)
  Booties - ¾ ounce, (20 grams, 75 yards)
Straight knitting needles, sizes 4 (3.50 mm)
  and 5 (3.75 mm) **or** sizes needed for
  gauge
Stitch holders - 3
Tapestry needle
Sewing needle and thread
⅝" Buttons - 5
⅜"w Ribbon - 1 yard for Bonnet
¼"w Ribbon - 1 yard for Booties
Blanket
Worsted Weight Yarn:
  36 ounces, (1,020 grams, 2,100 yards)
  24" Circular knitting needles, size
    10½ (6.50 mm) **or** size needed for gauge

GAUGE: In pattern, with Sport Weight Yarn and
  larger size needles, 22 sts and 30 rows = 4"
  In pattern, with two strands of Worsted
  Weight Yarn and circular needles,
  15 sts and 21 rows = 4½"

STITCH GUIDE

TWIST (uses 2 sts)
Knit the second stitch on left needle making sure
not to drop off needle **(Fig. 10a)**, then knit the
first stitch **(Fig. 10b)**, slipping both stitches off
needle.

Fig. 10a

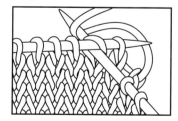

Fig. 10b

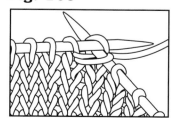

SACQUE

Sacque is worked in one piece to underarm.

BODY
With larger size needles, cast on 133 sts.

Rows 1-3: Knit across.

Row 4 (Buttonhole row)**:** K2, [YO **(Fig. 7a, page 2)**, K2 tog **(Fig. 1, page 1)** (buttonhole made)], knit across.

Work 3 more buttonholes in same manner every 2¼" to Right Front Neck Shaping.

Row 5: Knit across.

Row 6 (Right side)**:** K4, P1, work Twist, P1, K3, (P3, K3) across to last 8 sts, P1, work Twist, P1, K4.

Row 7: K5, P2, K1, P3, (K3, P3) across to last 8 sts, K1, P2, K5.

Rows 8 and 9: Repeat Rows 6 and 7.

Row 10: K4, P1, work Twist, P4, K3, (P3, K3) across to last 11 sts, P4, work Twist, P1, K4.

Row 11: K5, P2, K4, P3, (K3, P3) across to last 11 sts, K4, P2, K5.

Rows 12 and 13: Repeat Rows 10 and 11.

Repeat Rows 6-13 for pattern until Sacque measures approximately 7" from cast on edge, ending by working Row 13.

RIGHT FRONT
Row 1: K4, P1, work Twist, P1, (K3, P3) 4 times, slip next 63 sts onto st holder (Back), slip remaining 38 sts onto second st holder (Left Front): 32 sts.

Row 2: (K3, P3) 4 times, K1, P2, K5.

Row 3: K4, P1, work Twist, P1, (K3, P3) 4 times.

Row 4: (K3, P3) 4 times, K1, P2, K5.

To increase, knit into the front **and** into the back of next stitch.

Row 5: K4, P1, work Twist, (P2, increase) across to last st, P1: 40 sts.

Row 6: K1, P2, (K2, P2) across to last 5 sts, K5.

Row 7: K4, P1, work Twist, (P2, work Twist) across to last st, P1.

Repeat Rows 6 and 7 for pattern until Right Front measures approximately 9½" from cast on edge, ending by working Row 6.

Cut yarn.

Continued on page 9.

NECK SHAPING

Row 1: Slip first 15 sts onto st holder, (P2, work Twist) 6 times, P1: 25 sts.

Row 2: K1, (P2, K2) across.

Row 3: P2 tog *(Fig. 2, page 1)*, work Twist, (P2, work Twist) 5 times, P1: 24 sts.

Row 4: K1, P2, (K2, P2) 5 times, K1.

Row 5: Slip 1 as if to **knit**, K1, PSSO *(Fig. 4, page 2)*, K1, (P2, work Twist) 5 times, P1: 23 sts.

Row 6: K1, P2, (K2, P2) across.

Row 7: Slip 1 as if to **knit**, K1, PSSO, (P2, work Twist) 5 times, P1: 22 sts.

Row 8: K1, (P2, K2) 5 times, P1.

Row 9: P2 tog, P1, work Twist, (P2, work Twist) 4 times, P1: 21 sts.

Row 10: K1, (P2, K2) across.

Row 11: P2 tog, work Twist, (P2, work Twist) 4 times, P1: 20 sts.

Bind off remaining sts in pattern.

BACK

With **right** side facing, slip 63 sts from Back st holder onto larger size needle.

Row 1: Bind off 6 sts (armhole), K2, (P3, K3) across: 57 sts.

Row 2: P3, (K3, P3) across.

Row 3: K3, (P3, K3) across.

Row 4: P3, (K3, P3) across.

Row 5: P1, increase, (P2, increase) across to last st, P1: 76 sts.

Row 6: K1, P2, (K2, P2) across to last st, K1.

Row 7: P1, work Twist, (P2, work Twist) across to last st, P1.

Repeat Rows 6 and 7 for pattern until Back measures same as Right Front, ending by working Row 7.

Next Row: Bind off 20 sts, P2, (K2, P2) 8 times, K1, slip 36 sts just worked onto st holder, bind off remaining 20 sts.

LEFT FRONT

With **right** side facing, slip 38 sts from Left Front st holder onto larger size needle.

Row 1: Bind off 6 sts (armhole), P2, K3, (P3, K3) 3 times, P1, work Twist, P1, K4: 32 sts.

Row 2: K5, P2, K1, (P3, K3) across.

Row 3: (P3, K3) 4 times, P1, work Twist, P1, K4.

Row 4: K5, P2, K1, (P3, K3) across.

Row 5: P1, (increase, P2) 8 times, work Twist, P1, K4: 40 sts.

Row 6: K5, P2, (K2, P2) across to last st, K1.

Row 7: P1, work Twist, (P2, work Twist) 8 times, P1, K4.

Repeat Rows 6 and 7 for pattern until Left Front measures same as Right Front to Neck Shaping, ending by working Row 6.

NECK SHAPING

Row 1: P1, (work Twist, P2) 6 times, slip remaining 15 sts onto st holder: 25 sts.

Row 2: (K2, P2) across to last st, K1.

Row 3: P1, work Twist, (P2, work Twist) across to last 2 sts, P2 tog tbl *(Fig. 3, page 1)*: 24 sts.

Row 4: K1, P2, (K2, P2) across to last st, K1.

Row 5: P1, (work Twist, P2) 5 times, K1, K2 tog: 23 sts.

Row 6: P2, (K2, P2) across to last st, K1.

Row 7: P1, (work Twist, P2) 5 times, K2 tog: 22 sts.

Row 8: P1, (K2, P2) across to last st, K1.

Row 9: P1, work Twist, (P2, work Twist) across to last 3 sts, P1, P2 tog tbl: 21 sts.

Row 10: (K2, P2) across to last st, K1.

Row 11: P1, work Twist, (P2, work Twist) across to last 2 sts, P2 tog tbl: 20 sts.

Bind off remaining sts in pattern.

SLEEVE (Make 2)
CUFF
With larger size needles, cast on 36 sts **loosely**.

Rows 1-5: Knit across.

BODY
Row 1 (Right side)**:** (K3, P3) across.

Rows 2-4: (K3, P3) across.

Rows 5 and 6: (P3, K3) across.

Row 7 (Increase row)**:** Increase, P2, (K3, P3) across to last 3 sts, K2, increase: 38 sts.

Maintaining established pattern, continue to increase one stitch at **each** edge, every eighth row, 4 times **more**: 46 sts.

Work even until Sleeve measures approximately 6½" from cast on edge, ending by working a **wrong** side row.

Bind off all sts **loosely** in pattern.

FINISHING
Sew shoulder seams.

Weave underarm seam on each Sleeve *(Fig. 9, page 3)*.

Set in Sleeves, matching center of last row on Sleeve to shoulder seam and easing to fit opening.

NECK BAND
Row 1: With **right** side facing, slip 15 sts from Right Front st holder onto smaller size needle, K7, (K2 tog, K2) twice, pick up 7 sts along Right Front neck edge *(Figs. 8a & b, page 3)*, slip 36 sts from Back st holder onto empty needle, K3, K2 tog, (K2, K2 tog) 7 times, K3, pick up 7 sts along Left Front neck edge, slip 15 sts from Left Front st holder onto empty needle, (K2, K2 tog) twice, K7: 68 sts.

Row 2: Knit across.

Row 3 (Buttonhole row)**:** K2, YO, K2 tog, knit across.

Rows 4-6: Knit across.

Bind off all sts **loosely** in **knit**.

Sew buttons to Left Front.

BONNET
CROWN
With smaller size needles, cast on 56 sts.

Rows 1-5: Knit across.

Change to larger size needles.

Row 6 (Right side)**:** K4, (P3, K3) 3 times, P1, work Twist, P1, K4, P1, work Twist, P1, (K3, P3) 3 times, K4.

Row 7: P4, (K3, P3) 3 times, K1, P2, K6, P2, K1, (P3, K3) 3 times, P4.

Rows 8 and 9: Repeat Rows 6 and 7.

Row 10: P4, K3, (P3, K3) twice, P4, work Twist, P1, K4, P1, work Twist, P4, K3, (P3, K3) twice, P4.

Row 11: K4, P3, (K3, P3) twice, K4, P2, K6, P2, K4, P3, (K3, P3) twice, K4.

Rows 12 and 13: Repeat Rows 10 and 11.

Repeat Rows 6-13 for pattern until Crown measures approximately 4½" from cast on edge, ending by working a **right** side row.

BACK
Maintain established pattern.

Rows 1 and 2: Bind off 20 sts, work across: 16 sts.

Work even until Back measures approximately 4½", ending by working a **wrong** side row.

Slip sts onto st holder; cut yarn.

Sew sides of Back to bound off edges of Crown.

NECK BAND
Row 1: With **right** side facing and using smaller size needles, pick up 20 sts along first side of Crown *(Figs. 8a & b, page 3)*, slip 16 sts from Back st holder onto empty needle, K1, (K2 tog, K1) 5 times, pick up 20 sts along second side of Crown: 51 sts.

Rows 2-6: Knit across.

Bind off all sts in **knit**.

Sew an 18" length of ³⁄₈" wide ribbon to each corner of Bonnet for tie. Trim as desired.

Continued on page 13.

1

BOOTIES
CUFF

With smaller size needles, cast on 33 sts.

Rows 1-3: Knit across.

Change to larger size needles.

Row 4: K3, (P3, K3) across.

Row 5: P3, (K3, P3) across.

Row 6: K3, (P3, K3) across.

Rows 7 and 8: P3, (K3, P3) across.

Rows 9 and 10: Repeat Rows 4 and 5.

Rows 11 and 12: K3, (P3, K3) across.

Row 13: P3, (K3, P3) across.

Rows 14 and 15: Repeat Rows 4 and 5.

Change to smaller size needles.

Row 16 (Right side)**:** K1, (P1, K1) across.

Row 17: P1, (K1, P1) across.

Row 18 (Eyelet row)**:** K1, ★ P1, YO *(Fig. 7b, page 2)*, P2 tog *(Fig. 2, page 1)*, K1; repeat from ★ across.

Row 19: P1, (K1, P1) across.

Row 20: K1, (P1, K1) across.

INSTEP

Change to larger size needles.

Row 1: K 13, slip sts just worked onto st holder, (K1, increase) 3 times *(see Increases, page 1)*, K1, slip remaining 13 sts onto second st holder: 10 sts.

Knit every row until Instep measures approximately 1³/₄", ending by working a **wrong** side row.

Slip sts onto st holder; cut yarn.

SIDES

Row 1: With **right** side facing, slip 13 sts from first st holder onto larger size needle, pick up 7 sts along first side of Instep *(Figs. 8a & b, page 3)*, slip 10 sts from Instep st holder onto empty needle and knit across, pick up 7 sts along second side of Instep, slip 13 sts from last st holder onto empty needle and knit across: 50 sts.

Rows 2-9: Knit across.

Decrease Row: K 20, K2 tog *(Fig. 1, page 1)*, K6, K2 tog, K 20: 48 sts.

SOLE

Row 1: K 27, K2 tog, leave remaining 19 sts unworked, **turn**.

Rows 2-31: K7, K2 tog, leave remaining sts unworked, **turn**.

Row 32: K7, K2 tog, knit remaining 4 sts: 16 sts.

Bind off all sts in **knit**.

Weave back seam *(Fig. 9, page 3)*.

Sew back of Sole to Sides.

Weave an 18" length of ¹/₄" wide ribbon through eyelet row on each Bootie.

BLANKET
Finished Size: 36" x 45"

Blanket is worked holding two strands of yarn together.

Cast on 113 sts.

Rows 1-5: Knit across.

Row 6 (Right side)**:** K7, P3, (K3, P3) across to last 7 sts, K7.

Row 7: K4, P3, (K3, P3) across to last 4 sts, K4.

Row 8: K7, P3, (K3, P3) across to last 7 sts, K7.

Rows 9 and 10: K4, P3, (K3, P3) across to last 4 sts, K4.

Row 11: K7, P3, (K3, P3) across to last 7 sts, K7.

Row 12: K4, P3, (K3, P3) across to last 4 sts, K4.

Rows 13 and 14: K7, P3, (K3, P3) across to last 7 sts, K7.

Repeat Rows 7-14 for pattern until Blanket measures approximately 44" from cast on edge, ending by working Row 9 or Row 13.

Last 5 Rows: Knit across.

Bind off all sts.

3. WINSOME WHITE

Finished Size: 6 months

MATERIALS
Saceue, Bonnet, and Booties
Sport Weight Yarn:
   Sacque - 3¾ ounces,
      (110 grams, 380 yards)
   Bonnet - ¾ ounce, (20 grams, 75 yards)
   Booties - ¾ ounce, (20 grams, 75 yards)
Straight knitting needles, sizes 4 (3.50 mm)
   and 5 (3.75 mm) **or** sizes needed for
   gauge
Stitch holders - 3
Tapestry needle
Sewing needle and thread
⅝" Buttons - 5
⅜"w Ribbon - 1 yard for Bonnet
¼"w Ribbon - 1 yard for Booties
Blanket
Worsted Weight Yarn:
   32 ounces, (910 grams, 1,865 yards)
   29" Circular knitting needles, size
      10½ (6.50 mm) **or** size needed for gauge

GAUGE: In pattern, with Sport Weight Yarn and
larger size needles, 22 sts and 30 rows = 4"
In pattern, with two strands of Worsted
Weight Yarn and larger size circular
needles, 11 sts and 15 rows = 3½"

SACQUE
Sacque is worked in one piece to underarm.

RIBBING
With smaller size needles, cast on 137 sts.

Row 1: K1, (P1, K1) across.

Row 2: P1, (K1, P1) across.

Rows 3-5: Repeat Rows 1 and 2 once, then
repeat Row 1 once **more**.

BODY
Change to larger size needles.

Row 1 (Right side)**:** Knit across decreasing 22 sts
evenly spaced **(Fig. 1, page 1)**: 115 sts.

Row 2: Purl across.

Row 3: K2, K2 tog, ★ YO **(Fig. 7a, page 2)**, K2,
K2 tog; repeat from ★ across to last 3 sts, YO, K3.

Row 4: Purl across.

Row 5: Knit across.

Row 6: Purl across.

Row 7: K2 tog, (YO, K2, K2 tog) across to last st,
YO, K1.

Row 8: Purl across.

Row 9: Knit across.

Repeat Rows 2-9 for pattern until Sacque measures
approximately 7" from cast on edge, ending by
working Row 8.

RIGHT FRONT
Row 1: K 25, slip next 59 sts onto st holder
(Back), slip remaining 31 sts onto second st holder
(Left Front): 25 sts.

Row 2: Purl across.

Row 3: K2, K2 tog, (YO, K2, K2 tog) 5 times,
YO, K1.

Row 4: Purl across.

Row 5: Knit across.

Row 6: Purl across.

Row 7: K2 tog, (YO, K2, K2 tog) 5 times, YO,
K3.

Row 8: Purl across.

Row 9: Knit across.

Rows 10-21: Repeat Rows 2-9 once, then repeat
Rows 2-5 once **more**.

NECK SHAPING
Row 1: P 19, slip remaining 6 sts onto st holder:
19 sts.

Row 2: Slip 1 as if to **knit**, K1, PSSO **(Fig. 4,
page 2)**, K2 tog, (YO, K2, K2 tog) 3 times, YO,
K3: 18 sts.

Row 3: Purl across.

Row 4: Slip 1 as if to **knit**, K1, PSSO, knit across:
17 sts.

Row 5: Purl across.

Row 6: Slip 1 as if to **knit**, K1, PSSO, K2 tog,
(YO, K2, K2 tog) 3 times, YO, K1: 16 sts.

Row 7: Purl across.

Row 8: Slip 1 as if to **knit**, K1, PSSO, knit across:
15 sts.

Row 9: Purl across.

Bind off remaining sts in **knit**.

Continued on page 15.

BACK

With **right** side facing, slip 59 sts from Back st holder onto larger size needle.

Row 1: Bind off 6 sts (armhole), knit across: 53 sts.

Row 2: Purl across.

Row 3: K3, K2 tog, (YO, K2, K2 tog) across to last 4 sts, YO, K4.

Row 4: Purl across.

Row 5: Knit across.

Row 6: Purl across.

Row 7: K1, K2 tog, (YO, K2, K2 tog) across to last 2 sts, YO, K2.

Row 8: Purl across.

Row 9: Knit across.

Rows 10-30: Repeat Rows 2-9 twice, then repeat Rows 2-6 once **more**.

Row 31: Bind off 15 sts in **knit**, knit next 22 sts, slip 23 sts just worked onto st holder, bind off remaining 15 sts in **knit**.

LEFT FRONT

With **right** side facing, slip 31 sts from Left Front st holder onto larger size needle.

Row 1: Bind off 6 sts (armhole), knit across: 25 sts.

Row 2: Purl across.

Row 3: K2 tog, (YO, K2, K2 tog) 5 times, YO, K3.

Row 4: Purl across.

Row 5: Knit across.

Row 6: Purl across.

Row 7: K2, K2 tog, (YO, K2, K2 tog) 5 times, YO, K1.

Row 8: Purl across.

Row 9: Knit across.

Rows 10-20: Repeat Rows 2-9 once, then repeat Rows 2-4 once **more**.

NECK SHAPING

Row 1: K 19, slip remaining 6 sts onto st holder: 19 sts.

Row 2: Purl across.

Row 3: K2, K2 tog, (YO, K2, K2 tog) 3 times, YO, K1, K2 tog: 18 sts.

Row 4: Purl across.

Row 5: Knit across to last 2 sts, K2 tog: 17 sts.

Row 6: Purl across.

Row 7: K2 tog, (YO, K2, K2 tog) 3 times, YO, K1, K2 tog: 16 sts.

Row 8: Purl across.

Row 9: Knit across to last 2 sts, K2 tog: 15 sts.

Row 10: Purl across.

Bind off remaining sts in **knit**.

SLEEVE (Make 2)
RIBBING

With smaller size needles, cast on 34 sts **loosely**.

Work in K1, P1 ribbing for 5 rows increasing one stitch at end of last row **(see Increases, page 1)**: 35 sts.

BODY

Change to larger size needles.

Row 1 (Right side)**:** Knit across.

Row 2: Purl across.

Row 3: K2, K2 tog, (YO, K2, K2 tog) across to last 3 sts, YO, K3.

Row 4: Purl across.

Row 5: Knit across.

Row 6: Purl across.

Row 7 (Increase row)**:** Increase, K3, K2 tog, (YO, K2, K2 tog) across to last st, YO, increase: 37 sts.

Rows 8-10: Repeat Rows 4-6.

Row 11: K3, K2 tog, (YO, K2, K2 tog) across to last 4 sts, YO, K4.

Row 12: Purl across.

Row 13 (Increase row)**:** Increase, knit across to last st, increase: 39 sts.

Maintaining established pattern, continue to increase one stitch at **each** edge, every sixth row, once **more**; then increase every eighth row, twice: 45 sts.

Work even until Sleeve measures approximately 6½" from cast on edge, ending by working a **purl** row.

Bind off all sts **loosely** in **knit**.

FINISHING

Sew shoulder seams.

Weave underarm seam on each Sleeve **(Fig. 9, page 3)**.

Set in Sleeves, matching center of last row on Sleeve to shoulder seam and easing to fit opening.

NECK BAND

Row 1: With **right** side facing and using smaller size needles, knit 6 sts from Right Front st holder, pick up 11 sts along Right Front neck edge *(Figs. 8a & b, page 3)*, knit 23 sts from Back st holder, pick up 11 sts along Left Front neck edge, slip 6 sts from Left Front st holder onto empty needle and knit across: 57 sts.

Row 2: K1, (P1, K1) across.

Row 3: P1, (K1, P1) across.

Rows 4 and 5: Repeat Rows 2 and 3.

Bind off all sts **loosely** in **knit**.

LEFT FRONT BAND

With **right** side facing and using smaller size needles, pick up 66 sts along Neck Band and Left Front edge.

Work in K1, P1 ribbing for 5 rows.

Bind off all sts in **knit**.

RIGHT FRONT BAND

With **right** side facing and using smaller size needles, pick up 66 sts along Right Front and Neck Band edge.

Rows 1 and 2: (K1, P1) across.

Row 3 (Buttonhole row)**:** (K1, P1) twice, K1, **[**YO, K2 tog (buttonhole made)**]**, ★ (P1, K1) 6 times, YO, K2 tog; repeat from ★ 3 times **more**, P1, K1, P1.

Rows 4 and 5: (K1, P1) across.

Bind off all sts in **knit**.

Sew buttons to Left Front Band.

BONNET
CROWN
RIBBING

With smaller size needles, cast on 61 sts.

Row 1: K1, (P1, K1) across.

Row 2: P1, (K1, P1) across.

Rows 3-5: Repeat Rows 1 and 2 once, then repeat Row 1 once **more**.

BODY

Change to larger size needles.

Row 1 (Right side)**:** Knit across decreasing 8 sts evenly spaced *(Fig. 1, page 1)*: 53 sts.

Row 2: Purl across.

Row 3: K3, K2 tog, ★ YO *(Fig. 7a, page 2)*, K2, K2 tog; repeat from ★ across to last 4 sts, YO, K4.

Row 4: Purl across.

Row 5: Knit across.

Row 6: Purl across.

Row 7: K1, (K2 tog, YO, K2) across.

Row 8: Purl across.

Row 9: Knit across.

Rows 10-30: Repeat Rows 2-9 twice, then repeat Rows 2-6 once **more**.

BACK

Row 1: Bind off 19 sts, K1, (K2 tog, YO, K2) across: 34 sts.

Row 2: Bind off 19 sts, purl across: 15 sts.

Row 3: Knit across.

Row 4: Purl across.

Row 5: K2 tog, (YO, K2, K2 tog) 3 times, YO, K1.

Row 6: Purl across.

Row 7: Knit across.

Row 8: Purl across.

Row 9: K2, K2 tog, (YO, K2, K2 tog) twice, YO, K3.

Row 10: Purl across.

Rows 11-32: Repeat Rows 3-10 twice, then repeat Rows 3-8 once **more**.

Slip sts onto st holder; cut yarn.

Sew sides of Back to bound off edges of Crown.

NECK BAND

Row 1: With **right** side facing and using smaller size needles, pick up 22 sts along first side of Crown *(Figs. 8a & b, page 3)*, slip 15 sts from Back st holder onto empty needle, K1, (K2 tog 3 times, K1) twice, pick up 22 sts along second side of Crown: 53 sts.

Row 2: P1, (K1, P1) across.

Row 3: K1, (P1, K1) across.

Rows 4-6: Repeat Rows 2 and 3 once, then repeat Row 2 once **more**.

Bind off all sts in ribbing.

Sew an 18" length of ³/₈" wide ribbon to each corner of Bonnet for tie. Trim as desired.

Continued on page 17.

BOOTIES

CUFF

With larger size needles, cast on 36 sts.

Rows 1-3: (K1, P1) across.

Row 4 (Right side)**:** Increase *(see Increases, page 1)*, knit across: 37 sts.

Row 5: Purl across.

Row 6: K3, K2 tog *(Fig. 1, page 1)*, ★ YO *(Fig. 7a, page 2)*, K2, K2 tog; repeat from ★ across to last 4 sts, YO, K4.

Row 7: Purl across.

Row 8: Knit across.

Row 9: Purl across.

Row 10: K1, (K2 tog, YO, K2) across.

Row 11: Purl across.

Change to smaller size needles.

Row 12: K1, (P1, K1) across.

Row 13: P1, (K1, P1) across.

Row 14 (Eyelet row)**:** K1, (YO, K2 tog) across.

Row 15: P1, (K1, P1) across.

Row 16: K1, (P1, K1) across.

INSTEP

Change to larger size needles.

Row 1: P 13, slip sts just worked onto st holder, P4, P2 tog *(Fig. 2, page 1)*, P5, slip remaining 13 sts onto second st holder: 10 sts.

Beginning with a **knit** row, work 13 rows in Stockinette Stitch.

Slip sts onto st holder; cut yarn.

SIDES

With **right** side facing and using larger size needles, knit 13 sts from first st holder, pick up 7 sts along first side of Instep *(Figs. 8a & b, page 3)*, knit 10 sts from Instep st holder, pick up 7 sts along second side of Instep, slip 13 sts from last st holder onto empty needle and knit across: 50 sts.

Beginning with a **purl** row, work in Stockinette Stitch for 6 rows.

Decrease Row: P 20, P2 tog, P6, P2 tog, P 20: 48 sts.

SOLE

Row 1: K 27, K2 tog, leave remaining 19 sts unworked, **turn**.

Rows 2-31: K7, K2 tog, leave remaining sts unworked, **turn**.

Row 32: K7, K2 tog, knit remaining 4 sts: 16 sts.

Bind off all sts in **knit**.

Weave back seam *(Fig. 9, page 3)*.

Sew back of Sole to Sides.

Weave an 18" length of ¼" wide ribbon through eyelet row on each Bootie.

BLANKET

Finished Size: 34" x 45"

Blanket is worked holding two strands of yarn together.

Cast on 107 sts.

Rows 1-6: Knit across.

Row 7: K4, purl across to last 4 sts, K4.

Row 8 (Right side)**:** K6, K2 tog *(Fig. 1, page 1)*, ★ YO *(Fig. 7a, page 2)*, K2, K2 tog; repeat from ★ across to last 7 sts, YO, K7.

Row 9: K4, purl across to last 4 sts, K4.

Row 10: Knit across.

Row 11: K4, purl across to last 4 sts, K4.

Row 12: K4, K2 tog, (YO, K2, K2 tog) across to last 5 sts, YO, K5.

Row 13: K4, purl across to last 4 sts, K4.

Row 14: Knit across.

Row 15: K4, purl across to last 4 sts, K4.

Row 16: K6, K2 tog, (YO, K2, K2 tog) across to last 7 sts, YO, K7.

Repeat Rows 9-16 for pattern until Blanket measures approximately 44" from cast on edge, ending by working Row 9 or Row 13.

Last 6 Rows: Knit across.

Bind off all sts.

4. WONDERFULLY WHITE

Finished Size: 6 months

MATERIALS
Sacque, Bonnet, and Booties
Sport Weight Yarn:
Sacque - 3¾ ounces,
(110 grams, 380 yards)
Bonnet - ¾ ounce, (20 grams, 75 yards)
Booties - ¾ ounce, (20 grams, 75 yards)
Straight knitting needles, sizes 4 (3.50 mm)
and 5 (3.75 mm) **or** sizes needed for gauge
Stitch holders - 3
Tapestry needle
Sewing needle and thread
⅝" Buttons - 3
⅜"w Ribbon - 1 yard for Bonnet
¼"w Ribbon - 1 yard for Booties
Blanket
Worsted Weight Yarn:
32 ounces, (910 grams, 1,865 yards)
29" Circular knitting needles, size
10½ (6.50 mm) **and** 11 (8.00 mm) **or**
sizes needed for gauge

GAUGE: With Sport Weight Yarn and
larger size needles, in Stockinette
Stitch, 22 sts and 30 rows = 4"
In pattern, 5 repeats and 28 rows = 3½"
In pattern, with two strands of Worsted
Weight Yarn and larger size circular
needles, 11 sts and 15 rows = 3½"

SACQUE
Sacque is worked in one piece to underarm.

RIBBING
With smaller size needles, cast on 122 sts.

Rows 1-4: K2, (P1, K1) across.

BODY
Change to larger size needles.

Row 1 (Right side)**:** K4, P1, (K3, P1) across to last st, K1.

Row 2: K2, (P3, K1) across.

See Yarn Overs, page 2.

Row 3: K1, ★ YO, slip 1 as if to **knit**, K2 tog, PSSO **(Figs. 6a & b, page 2)**, YO, P1; repeat from ★ across to last st, K1.

Row 4: K2, (P3, K1) across.

Rows 5-48: Repeat Rows 1-4, 11 times.

Row 49: K3, K2 tog, (K6, K2 tog) 14 times, K5: 107 sts.

LEFT FRONT
Row 1: P 24, slip next 55 sts onto st holder (Back), slip remaining 28 sts onto second st holder (Right Front): 24 sts.

Row 2: (P1, K1) across.

Row 3: Purl across.

Row 4: Knit across.

Row 5: Purl across.

Rows 6-18: Repeat Rows 2-5, 3 times; then repeat Row 2 once **more**.

NECK SHAPING
Row 1: P8, slip sts just worked onto st holder, purl across: 16 sts.

Row 2: Knit across to last 3 sts, K2 tog **(Fig. 1, page 1)**, K1: 15 sts.

Row 3: Purl across.

Row 4: (P1, K1) 6 times, P2 tog **(Fig. 2, page 1)**, K1: 14 sts.

Row 5: Purl across.

Row 6: Knit across to last 3 sts, K2 tog, K1: 13 sts.

Row 7: Purl across.

Row 8: P1, (K1, P1) across.

Row 9: Purl across.

Row 10: Knit across.

Rows 11-13: Repeat Rows 7-9.

Bind off remaining sts in **knit**.

BACK
With **wrong** side facing, slip 55 sts from Back st holder onto larger size needle.

Row 1: Bind off 4 sts (armhole), purl across: 51 sts.

Row 2: P1, (K1, P1) across.

Row 3: Purl across.

Row 4: Knit across.

Row 5: Purl across.

Rows 6-31: Repeat Rows 2-5, 6 times; then repeat Rows 2 and 3 once **more**.

Row 32: Bind off 13 sts in **knit**, knit next 24 sts, slip 25 sts just worked onto st holder, bind off remaining 13 sts in **knit**.

Continued on page 19.

RIGHT FRONT
With **wrong** side facing, slip 28 sts from Right Front st holder onto larger size needle.

Row 1: Bind off 4 sts (armhole), purl across: 24 sts.

Row 2: (K1, P1) across.

Row 3: Purl across.

Row 4: Knit across.

Row 5: Purl across.

Rows 6-18: Repeat Rows 2-5, 3 times; then repeat Row 2 once **more**.

NECK SHAPING
Row 1: Purl across to last 8 sts, slip last 8 sts onto st holder: 16 sts.

Row 2: K1, slip 1 as if to **knit**, K1, PSSO *(Fig. 4, page 2)*, knit across: 15 sts.

Row 3: Purl across.

Row 4: K1, P2 tog, (K1, P1) across: 14 sts.

Row 5: Purl across.

Row 6: K1, slip 1 as if to **knit**, K1, PSSO, knit across: 13 sts.

Row 7: Purl across.

Row 8: P1, (K1, P1) across.

Row 9: Purl across.

Row 10: Knit across.

Rows 11-13: Repeat Rows 7-9.

Bind off remaining sts in **knit**.

SLEEVE (Make 2)
RIBBING
With smaller size needles, cast on 30 sts **loosely**.

Work in K1, P1 ribbing for 5 rows.

BODY
Change to larger size needles.

Row 1: Knit across increasing 4 sts evenly spaced *(see Increases, page 1)*: 34 sts.

Row 2: Purl across.

Row 3: (K1, P1) across.

Row 4: Purl across.

Row 5: Knit across.

Rows 6-8: Repeat Rows 2-4.

Row 9 (Increase row)**:** Increase, knit across to last 2 sts, increase, K1: 36 sts.

Row 10: Purl across.

Row 11: (P1, K1) across.

Row 12: Purl across.

Row 13: Knit across.

Rows 14-16: Repeat Rows 10-12.

Row 17 (Increase row)**:** Increase, knit across to last 2 sts, increase, K1: 38 sts.

Rows 18-33: Repeat Rows 2-17: 42 sts.

Repeat Rows 2-5 for pattern until Sleeve measures approximately 6½" from cast on edge, ending by working a **purl** row.

Bind off all sts **loosely** in **knit**.

FINISHING
Sew shoulder seams.

Weave underarm seam on each Sleeve *(Fig. 9, page 3)*.

Set in Sleeves, matching center of last row on Sleeve to shoulder seam and easing to fit opening.

NECK BAND
Row 1: With **right** side facing and using smaller size needles, knit 8 sts from Right Front st holder, pick up 11 sts along Right Front neck edge *(Figs. 8a & b, page 3)*, knit 25 sts from Back st holder, pick up 11 sts along Left Front neck edge, slip 8 sts from Left Front st holder onto empty needle and knit across: 63 sts.

Row 2: K1, (P1, K1) across.

Row 3: P1, (K1, P1) across.

Rows 4 and 5: Repeat Rows 2 and 3.

Bind off all sts **loosely** in ribbing.

LEFT FRONT BAND
With **right** side facing and using smaller size needles, pick up 67 sts evenly spaced along Neck Band and Left Front edge.

Row 1: K1, (P1, K1) across.

Row 2: P1, (K1, P1) across.

Rows 3 and 4: Repeat Rows 1 and 2.

Bind off all sts in **knit**.

RIGHT FRONT BAND

With **right** side facing and using smaller size needles, pick up 67 sts evenly spaced along Right Front edge and Neck Band.

Row 1: K1, (P1, K1) across.

Row 2 (Buttonhole row): (P1, K1) 19 times, ★ [YO, K2 tog (buttonhole made)], (P1, K1) 5 times; repeat from ★ once **more**, YO, K2 tog, P1, K1, P1.

Row 3: K1, (P1, K1) across.

Row 4: P1, (K1, P1) across.

Bind off all sts in **knit**.

Sew buttons to Left Front Band.

BONNET
CROWN
RIBBING

With smaller size needles, cast on 66 sts.

Work in K1, P1 ribbing for 5 rows.

BODY

Change to larger size needles.

Row 1 (Right side): K4, P1, (K3, P1) across to last st, K1.

Row 2: K2, (P3, K1) across.

See Yarn Overs, page 2.

Row 3: K1, ★ YO, slip 1 as if to **knit**, K2 tog, PSSO *(Figs. 6a & b, page 2)*, YO, P1; repeat from ★ across to last st, K1.

Row 4: K2, (P3, K1) across.

Rows 5-28: Repeat Rows 1-4, 6 times.

BACK

Row 1: Bind off 24 sts, (K3, P1) across to last st, K1: 42 sts.

Row 2: Bind off 24 sts, K1, (P3, K1) across: 18 sts.

Row 3: K1, (YO, slip 1 as if to **knit**, K2 tog, PSSO, YO, P1) across to last st, K1.

Row 4: K2, (P3, K1) across.

Row 5: P1, (K3, P1) across to last st, K1.

Row 6: K2, (P3, K1) across.

Rows 7-36: Repeat Rows 3-6, 7 times; then repeat Rows 3 and 4 once **more**.

Slip sts onto st holder; cut yarn.

Sew sides of Back to bound off edges of Crown.

NECK BAND

Row 1: With **right** side facing and using smaller size needles, pick up 21 sts along first side of Crown *(Figs. 8a & b, page 3)*, slip 18 sts from Back st holder onto empty needle, K2 tog 9 times, pick up 21 sts along second side of Crown: 51 sts.

Row 2: K1, (P1, K1) across.

Row 3: P1, (K1, P1) across.

Rows 4-6: Repeat Rows 2 and 3 once, then repeat Row 2 once **more**.

Bind off all sts in ribbing.

Sew an 18" length of ³/₈" wide ribbon to each corner of Bonnet for tie. Trim as desired.

BOOTIES
CUFF

With smaller size needles, cast on 34 sts.

Rows 1-3: (K1, P1) across.

Change to larger size needles.

Row 4 (Right side): K4, P1, (K3, P1) across to last st, K1.

Row 5: K2, (P3, K1) across.

See Yarn Overs, page 2.

Row 6: K1, ★ YO, slip 1 as if to **knit**, K2 tog, PSSO *(Figs. 6a & b, page 2)*, YO, P1; repeat from ★ across to last st, K1.

Row 7: K2, (P3, K1) across.

Rows 8-16: Repeat Rows 4-7 twice, then repeat Row 4 once **more**.

Change to smaller size needles.

Rows 17 and 18: (K1, P1) across.

Row 19 (Eyelet row): K1, (YO, K2 tog) across to last st, K1.

Rows 20 and 21: (K1, P1) across.

Continued on page 21.

INSTEP

Change to larger size needles.

Row 1: K 13, slip sts just worked onto st holder, K1, increase *(see Increases, page 1)*, K4, increase, K1, slip remaining 13 sts onto second st holder: 10 sts.

Row 2: Purl across.

Row 3: (K1, P1) across.

Row 4: Purl across.

Row 5: Knit across.

Rows 6-14: Repeat Rows 2-5 twice, then repeat Row 2 once **more**.

Slip sts onto st holder; cut yarn.

SIDES

Row 1: With **right** side facing and using larger size needles, slip 13 sts from first st holder onto needle, pick up 7 sts along first side of Instep *(Figs. 8a & b, page 3)*, slip 10 sts from Instep st holder onto empty needle, (K1, P1) 5 times, pick up 7 sts along second side of Instep, slip 13 sts from last st holder onto empty needle and knit across: 50 sts.

Row 2: Purl across.

Row 3: Knit across.

Row 4: Purl across.

Row 5: (K1, P1) across.

Rows 6-8: Repeat Rows 2-4.

Row 9: Knit across.

Row 10: P 20, P2 tog *(Fig. 2, page 1)*, P6, P2 tog, P 20: 48 sts.

SOLE

Row 1: K 27, K2 tog, leave remaining 19 sts unworked, **turn**.

Rows 2-31: K7, K2 tog, leave remaining sts unworked, **turn**.

Row 32: K7, K2 tog, knit remaining 4 sts: 16 sts.

Bind off all sts in **knit**.

Weave back seam *(Fig. 9, page 3)*.

Sew back of Sole to Sides.

Weave an 18" length of ¼" wide ribbon through eyelet row on each Bootie.

BLANKET

Finished Size: 39" x 45"

Blanket is worked holding two strands of yarn together.

With smaller size circular needles, cast on 125 sts.

Rows 1-5: Knit across.

Change to larger size circular needles.

Row 6 (Right side)**:** K4, P1, (K3, P1) across to last 4 sts, K4.

Row 7: K5, P3, (K1, P3) across to last 5 sts, K5.

See Yarn Overs, page 2.

Row 8: K4, P1, ★ YO, slip 1 as if to **knit**, K2 tog, PSSO *(Figs. 6a & b, page 2)*, YO, P1; repeat from ★ across to last 4 sts, K4.

Row 9: K5, P3, (K1, P3) across to last 5 sts, K5.

Repeat Rows 6-9 for pattern until Blanket measures approximately 44" from cast on edge, ending by working Row 9.

Change to smaller size circular needles.

Last 6 Rows: Knit across.

Bind off all sts.